HYPNOTHERAPY FOUNDATION COURSE

The Student's Introduction to Hypnotherapy.

Hypnotherapy Foundation Course

First published 2012

ISBN-13: 978-1-904928-05-8
ISBN-10: 1-904928-05-6

www.copelandandwickson.com

The contents of this book are for educational purposes only. The
publishers, editors, and authors cannot accept any responsibility for
consequences arising from the use of information contained within
this book.

COURSE STRUCTURE

Welcome to the Hypnotherapy Foundation Course! Your course consists of 5 self-study modules which will guide you through your task of gaining an overview of the principles and practice of hypnotherapy. The content and a brief description of each module is given below.

MODULE 1 – What is hypnotherapy?

This module defines the subject and will provide you with some background information about the nature of the topic.

Module 1 contains the following sections:

What is hypnosis?
Everyday forms of trance
Misconceptions about hypnosis
Trance phenomena
A potted history of hypnosis

MODULE 2 – The hypnotherapist

This module examines the work and the role of the hypnotherapist.

Module 2 contains the following sections:

The unconscious mind
What is a hypnotherapist?
Clinical hypnotherapy
Analytical hypnotherapy

MODULE 3 – Therapeutic techniques

This module introduces the principal hypnotic techniques which are employed by the hypnotherapist when treating clients.

Module 3 contains the following sections:

Eliciting client information
Trance-induction
Self-hypnosis
Therapeutic suggestion
Therapeutic metaphor

MODULE 4 – Counselling techniques

This module introduces the general counselling techniques which are employed by the hypnotherapist when treating clients.

Module 4 contains the following sections:

Belief restructuring
Stress management counselling

MODULE 5 – Self-development techniques

This module introduces a number of self-development techniques which are employed by the hypnotherapist when treating clients.

Module 5 contains the following sections:

Neuro-linguistic programming
Positive thinking
Assertiveness

COURSE FORMAT

In each module you will find sections of reading matter accompanied by a series of Self-Assessment Questions.

These questions are designed to aid your understanding of the material which you have previously studied and should act as a checklist to ensure that you have grasped the main elements of what you have read.

HYPNOTHERAPY FOUNDATION

MODULE 1
WHAT IS HYPNOTHERAPY?

CONTENTS

What is hypnosis?

Everyday forms of trance

Misconceptions about hypnosis

Trance phenomena

- Breathing-rate changes

- Pupil dilation

- Muscular relaxation

- Body temperature changes

- Bodily sensations

- A potted history of hypnosis

WHAT IS HYPNOSIS?

Most writers shy away from a definitive definition of hypnosis because hypnosis is an individual perception of a naturally and uniquely occurring phenomenon which man has utilised in various forms for centuries.

Attempts at a definition have been put forward by modern writers as given below:

Here are two definitions which seem to explain the effects of the phenomenon.

Hypnosis is a state of mind in which suggestions are acted upon much more powerfully than is possible under normal conditions. While in hypnosis, one suppresses the power of conscious criticism. One's focus of attention is narrower and one's level of awareness on a focal point is much higher than if one were awake. During this heightened focus and awareness, suggestions appear to go directly into the unconscious mind.
Brian M Alman and Peter Lambrou
Self-Hypnosis

Under hypnosis, a person has control of more than his selectivity, or will power; he is in control of all his faculties except one. He can hear, see, feel, smell, taste and speak. Though he may sometimes look unconscious, he is completely aware and can therefore co-operate. The single exception to this control is what I call the critical faculty. If you give a suggestion which pleases an individual and which seems emotionally and morally reasonable to them, they will accept it despite the fact that under ordinary circumstances they might consider it an impossible suggestion.

Dave Elman
Hypnotherapy

To illustrate the point about the difficulty in formulating an accurate and universally-accepted definition, consider the comment given below:

Hypnosis as a word has been overused to the point of being robbed of any real meaning. When one word comes to describe as many different experiences as "hypnosis" has, there is ample opportunity for misunderstanding, mislabelling, misconception, and, ultimately, confusion. To date, there is no commonly accepted definition of hypnosis, nor does one seem forthcoming.

Michael D Yapko
Essentials of Hypnosis

Finally, perhaps the following remarks may be borne in mind when considering a definition of hypnosis:

It is precisely because hypnosis is one word for so many different experiences that the average person comes to believe that "hypnosis is hypnosis", regardless of the context in which it is applied.

Michael D Yapko
Essentials of Hypnosis

At a practical level it would be better to settle for a definition such as:

'A state of relaxation and concentration, at one with a state of heightened awareness, induced by suggestion; a non-additive power for good, and a natural manifestation of the mind at work'.
Neil French
Successful Hypnotherapy

From these statements and theories, therefore, we can attempt to define its characteristics by deducing that hypnosis is a state in which the subject:

- becomes reflective, contemplative and inward-looking

- clearly focuses on internal thoughts, images, emotions and bodily sensations

- is relaxed but inwardly alert and internally focused

- suspended conscious awareness

- can minimise external distractions

- consigns logical thought, deductive reasoning, rationality, problem-solving and the cares of the day to insignificance

- prefers creative, imaginative and symbolic imagery to that of tangible elements

- is inclined to be susceptible to external suggestions, proposals and propositions from which benefit can be derived

- often completely loses track of time

- may have little or no immediate recollection of what occurred or what was said during the trance-state

In fact it has been said that the hypnotic state is merely an altered state of consciousness – rather than an unconscious state – either when it is naturally occurring or when a therapist has formally induced it.

In summary, therefore, we often regard hypnosis as:

A frame of mind, open to suggestion.

SELF-ASSESSMENT QUESTIONS

- Why are experts and writers often reluctant to give a definitive definition of hypnosis?

- What is the significance of suggestion in hypnosis?

- What are the general characteristics of the hypnotic experience?

- Why do you think that one loses track of time when in a hypnotic state?

- What happens to your conscious reasoning powers when in a hypnotic state?

- Would you agree that one is relaxed and yet alert in a state of hypnosis?

EVERYDAY FORMS OF TRANCE

Because the hypnotic trance-state is a naturally occurring phenomenon it can be experienced by anyone in everyday life.

Consider the following remarks put forward about the trance-state:

Nearly everyone has experienced a trance-like state many times – though they might not have called it hypnosis. Have you ever caught yourself daydreaming and not noticed routine things happening around you?

Have you ever been absorbed reading a book or engrossed in an intricate project and not heard someone speak to you or not noticed how much time passed?

Perhaps you have had the experience of being so engrossed in a movie that you realised that it was almost over and yet it did not seem like over an hour and a half had passed. Or, you may have been driving on the freeway, absorbed in your thoughts, and then noticed that you had missed your exit. These are hypnotic-like trances.

Brian M Alman and Peter Lambrou
Self-Hypnosis

From this it is clear that each one of us in our everyday life can and does experience varying forms of trance on a regular basis. Consider for yourself some examples of trance in the waking or semi-waking state:

Do you know what it feels like to be half-asleep – in that

drowsy state between light sleep and full waking consciousness?

Do you know what it feels like to indulge in daydreaming?

Do you know what it feels like to allow your mind to wander?

Have you ever been lost in your own thoughts while driving, cycling or walking along the road and then arrived at your destination with no conscious recollection of your journey?

Have you ever become totally absorbed in a creative activity or interesting hobby to the exclusion of everything else around you?

Have you ever been in a situation in which you were 100 per cent, single-mindedly, internally focused on a task or a project?

Even if you have not experienced formally-induced trance, you will have, unknowingly, entered a state of hypnosis perhaps when relaxing at the end of an aerobics class or while doing some yoga exercises or while taking part in group meditation.

SELF-ASSESSMENT QUESTIONS

- How frequently do you catch yourself daydreaming in the course of a day?

- What kind of creative activities do you do regularly in which a trance-like state is induced?

- What kind of physical activities do you undertake regularly in which a trance-like state is induced?

- Explain why you believe that hypnosis is a naturally occurring phenomenon.

MISCONCEPTIONS ABOUT HYPNOSIS

It follows, therefore, that because of the difficulty in defining hypnosis, the phenomenon is surrounded by myths arising from a whole collection of half-truths unwittingly passed on by those in ignorance.

Some writers have sought to eradicate ignorance about the hypnotic state as given below:

As modern science brings technological enlightenment to this world, it's high time to bring hypnosis out of the dark ages and shine light of truth on its secrets. Let's rip away once and for all the shroud of mysticism that has surrounded this art for so many centuries. And let's begin by exposing the biggest secret of all: the power is NOT in the hypnotist; it is in the client – the person who is guided into hypnosis!
C Roy Hunter
The Art of Hypnotherapy

It is common for people to disbelieve that they have been hypnotised the first time or two it occurs. The reason is that the hypnotic trance is not a completely unique feeling. The absorption you may feel is familiar. Hypnosis is not a form of sleep, though a person in a trance often appears to be asleep. Actually, the opposite is true. The brain-wave patterns of people in hypnosis show alert wakefulness.
Brian M Alman and Peter Lambrou
Self-Hypnosis.

There is nothing magical about hypnosis at all, so it follows that there can be nothing magical about any cure or relief it helps create – in fact, hypnosis is a perfectly natural phenomenon occurring in man and animals, and is as much a part of our functioning, as are seeing and hearing.
Neil French
Successful Hypnotherapy

Despite the efforts of scientific writers and researchers, hypnosis has been wearing a cloak of mysticism for centuries. The very term hypnosis, derived from a Greek root word meaning sleep, is misleading. Hypnosis is related to sleep as night is to day – and is no more like it than night is like day. If you will put aside all preconceived notions and examine hypnosis clinically, you will find that it doesn't look, or "behave", as you thought it would.
Dave Elman
Hypnotherapy

If you are a newcomer to experiencing the hypnotic trance-state be assured that the following is a list of some popular misconceptions about formally induced hypnosis and the trance-state:

- the subject goes to sleep or into a kind of sleep

- the hypnotist has total control of the subject's mind

- the subject can remember nothing at all of what

happened in the trance-state

- the subject is completely unaware of what is going on around them

- if the hypnotist were to walk away the subject would not be able to return to the conscious waking state

- the subject is unable to open their eyes when in hypnosis

- people with strong, active, intelligent minds cannot be hypnotised

- some people are incapable of experiencing hypnosis

Often the above misconceptions of this naturally occurring phenomenon are related to the subject's fear of themselves or of their own power or, simply, a fear of the unknown.

SELF-ASSESSMENT QUESTIONS

- Why do you think that a number of myths and misconceptions surround the subject of hypnosis?

- Do you fall asleep when in a hypnotic state?

- Do you ever lose control of your faculties when in a hypnotic state?

- Can people who are intelligent and wise be hypnotised successfully?

- Do you know of anyone who is incapable of experiencing the trance state?

- Why do you think that some people hold mistaken beliefs about the subject of hypnosis?

TRANCE PHENOMENA

Let us now consider the way in which the trance-state manifests itself in order to assist your understanding of the phenomenon.

If you were an onlooker, you might observe the following signs when a subject entered the trance-state:

Breathing-rate changes

The subject's breathing rate may become shallower although they may sigh once or twice when becoming relaxed and releasing tension.

Pupil dilation

Sometimes the subject may stare fixedly at an object or merely stare without seeing anything. Often, at this stage, the subject's pupils will dilate which denotes that they are entering the trance-state.

Muscular relaxation

The subject's facial muscles will tend to smooth out and often the jaw will begin to drop.

Certainly most trance-subjects will, sooner or later, want to close their eyes.

The subject's limbs may become floppy.

The subject's eyelids may flutter or blink slowly or water

when closed – all signs of muscular relaxation.

The subject may have the desire to swallow repeatedly.

Body temperature changes

Some hypnotic subjects will flush or blush when entering hypnosis or at a point when significant emotional sensations are being experienced.

Bodily sensations

The subject may experience a whole range of bodily sensations associated with relaxation. For example, a tingling in the limbs, a general feeling of lightness or heaviness, a feeling of being detached from one's body.

In some cases, certain muscles – such as those muscles in the arms or legs – may jerk involuntarily. Alternatively, the subject may be affected by a seeming inability or disinclination to move due to muscular rigidity.

SELF-ASSESSMENT QUESTIONS

- What might you observe about a person's breathing while they are in hypnosis?

- When in a trance-state what might an onlooker observe about the subject's ability to relax physically?

- When observing a person in trance how might you detect a body temperature change?

- When you enter trance do you feel heaviness or lightness in your body?

- Have you ever experienced a desire not to want to move or a seeming inability to move?

A POTTED HISTORY OF HYPNOSIS

Although hypnosis is currently gaining favour and recognition in our modern society, the phenomenon has been around and has been utilised through the ages to assist mankind in various ways. It has not only been used therapeutically but also for the purposes of entertainment and attempted exploitation of people. In this course, however, we are solely concerned with the beneficial uses of hypnosis as an aid to treating those in need.

An encapsulated version of the history of hypnosis through the ages with regard to using hypnosis as a therapeutic tool is given below.

There is evidence that the Greeks and the Romans in ancient times adopted methods of treatment which resemble those employed in hypnotherapy today. However, the history of hypnosis as we know it and appreciate it today is commonly considered to have dated from the time of Dr Franz Mesmer (1734-1815) – a Viennese physician.

Mesmer experimented with his theory of utilising a *universal fluid* by means of magnets in order to channel healing energy into his patients. He described his cures as *animal magnetism* and his method of treatment became known as *mesmerism*. You will, of course, recognise both terms as having been freely incorporated into our language today.

Later the concept was taken up by a British physician, Dr James Braid (1795-1860), who coined the term hypnosis as a means of describing the sleep-like state induced in his patients. Braid laid the foundations for modern theories of hypnosis because he adhered to the belief that the trance-state was a product of the mind.

A French physician, Dr Jean-Martin Charcot (1825-1893), who worked at the Salpêtrière Hospital School in France, furthered the cause by taking an interest in the phenomenon. Charcot, however, believed that the hypnotic state was a pathological phenomenon and thus started a debate between those physicians who believed in the mind theory and those who subscribed to the body theory.

The school of thought supporting the body theory (or Salpêtrière school of thought) was headed by Charcot at the Hospital school and his followers also believed that the trance-state could only be achieved by hysteric patients.

The adherents to the *mind theory* (or Nancy school of thought) were principally Dr Ambroise-Auguste Liébeault (1823-1904) and Professor Hippolyte Bernheim (1843-1919) who both worked in Nancy in France. These doctors and their followers developed the ideas originally put forward by Braid.

The theory of hypnosis eventually attracted the attention of the famous Dr Sigmund Freud (1856-1939) – the man who invented psychoanalysis. Freud, however, finally

rejected hypnosis as a therapeutic medium and –
because of this – treatment using hypnosis was largely
ignored or discredited by the medical profession for
some time until the early part of this century.

During the 1914-1918 war, a shortage of psychiatrists
and the urgent need to treat shell-shocked patients
caused a review of the topic and a revival of the
application of its principles.

Also, at about this time, a French pharmacist, Emile
Coué (1857-1926), developed the idea of auto-
suggestion. His well-known phrase:

*Every day and in every way I am becoming better and
better*

This has also become a popular catch-phrase in our
language.

By the 1950s hypnotism was firmly established as a
method of treatment for patients with neurotic conditions.
Legislation was brought in by the Hypnotism Act of 1952
which strictly defined the conditions under which
hypnosis may be used in public demonstrations – thus
firmly separating the therapeutic community from the
practices of the stage hypnotist.

Today modern hypnotherapy has carefully selected
techniques from those used by its early practitioners and
modified such methods to accommodate the needs of
today's client. Hypnotherapy is now a well established
branch of complementary medicine and is widely

recognised by the medical profession as an effective tool for the treatment of patients with emotional and psychological disorders.

SELF-ASSESSMENT QUESTIONS

- Who was Dr Franz Mesmer?

- What contribution did Mesmer make to the development of hypnosis as we know it today?

- Who coined the term hypnosis taken from the Greek word for sleep?

- Who was the head of the Salpêtrière school of thought which adhered to the doctrine that hypnosis is a physical or pathological state?

- Who were the founders of the Nancy school of thought that adhered to the doctrine that hypnosis is a product of the mind?

- For what common catch-phrase is Emile Coué best known?

- What were the main provisions of the Hypnotism Act of 1952?

- How is hypnotherapy regarded today?

MODULE 2
THE HYPNOTHERAPIST

The unconscious mind

- Emotions

- Imagination

- Memory

- Behaviour and motivations

- Bodily functions

What is a hypnotherapist?

- Clinical hypnotherapy

- Smoking cessation

- Simple phobias

- Weight management

- Unwanted habits

- Confidence-building

- Performance enhancement

- Pain management

- Stress management

Analytical hypnotherapy

THE UNCONSCIOUS MIND

Hypnotherapy works by gaining direct access into the client's unconscious mind in order to remedy emotional disorders, to resolve psychological conflict, to eliminate unwanted habits and to modify destructive tendencies, behaviour and motivations.

Let us now consider some of the functions of the unconscious mind in order to be able to appreciate the critical significance of this part of the human organism and its role in the therapeutic process.

The unconscious mind is that part of our mind which is the core of our instincts and the very essence of our being. The unconscious mind, therefore, generates our emotions, houses our memory, manifests our creative and imaginative resources and dictates our behaviour and motivations.

Emotions

The unconscious mind is the seat of our emotions controlled and orchestrated by the autonomic nervous system (or involuntary nervous system).

Emotions may be either positive or negative according to whether they bring us joy or cause us distress.

Positive emotions are those of happiness, harmony, peace, love, contentment and excitement to name but a few.

Negative emotions may be those generated by fear such as anxiety, tension, worry, suspicion, embarrassment, guilt and shame. Or by sorrow such as sadness, grief, misery, remorse and loneliness. Or by anger such as fury, bitterness, resentment, boredom, discontent, frustration and jealousy.

Imagination

The unconscious mind is also responsible for giving birth to our creativity because it stimulates our imagination. Imagination thus gives rise to creative imagery, artistic talents, flexible thinking, intuition and any psychic qualities, which we may possess.

Memory

The unconscious mind absorbs information through our senses of sight, hearing, touch, taste and smell and all images or impulses are then processed by the brain. It has been said that everything we experience is, at some level, recorded by the unconscious mind and is then consigned to our memory banks. In this way, all our experiences are recorded by the unconscious mind for later retrieval when necessary.

When we are children, this record of our experiences is made to enable us to grow up in safety by assisting the learning process and by alerting us to possible dangers. If a child is taught how to read and write it will have a better chance of interacting with people in society in adulthood and this education will also enable them to become independent of their family when the time comes to spread their wings.

If a child learns about danger either when being instructed by parents or, perhaps, when learning the hard way, these lessons will be used for future reference for their own protection. The rationality behind this process is that the unconscious mind always strives to free itself of unnecessary burdens of thought so that its scarce energy resources are not overloaded or encumbered unnecessarily.

If information and learning is consigned to the unconscious mind and tagged for ease of retrieval, the conscious mind will then be free to cope with day-to-day emergencies and with situations which require logical and reasoned thinking.

Those things which we remember most readily are obviously those things which have the most impact on our lives and which affect our emotions profoundly in some way. In some cases, however, if we experience what we perceive as an unbearable trauma or a life-threatening danger, we may find that such disturbing events will often be ignored or temporarily forgotten by the conscious mind.

Such memories are swept away into the recesses of the unconscious mind because they are too unpleasant for the conscious mind to deal with at the time. The process of consigning material to the unconscious mind ready for retrieval will, thus, have been interrupted. This will mean that the individual is not easily able to retrieve such information on demand and, therefore, the mind will be put into a conflict-situation.

If a memory is buried in the unconscious mind and is not readily accessible to the conscious mind, then it is said to have become **repressed**. A repressed memory will cause a degree of unpleasant, emotional distress for the sufferer and this will often result in distressing emotional symptoms.

This conflict-state will usually mean that the individual will need help from a therapist in order to retrieve the memory and to resolve the associated traumatic effects of the incident.

The act of repression is again a naturally-occurring phenomenon which happens in our daily life. For example, if you bang your elbow or stub your toe you often think you can make the pain go away by trying not to think about it. However, you are unlikely to eliminate pain in such a way and, even if you do succeed, the relief is likely to be only temporary.

With a more serious injury the pain will endure until it is treated satisfactorily – returning again and again until relief is obtained. It can be likened to a cough or a sneeze or a smile – if you strive to suppress it, it will return with force and vigour.

A suppressed tickle in the throat can turn into a loud cough, a stifled irritation in the nose can turn into a bout of sneezing and a veiled smirk may transform itself into an uncontrollable fit of the giggles.

Behaviour and motivations

Because of the way in which information is stored in the unconscious mind, our behaviour and our motivations will be influenced by our previous experiences. For example, when a child is taught how to dress or how to behave in an acceptable manner on social occasions at any early age, then that child will automatically incorporate this early-learning experience into their behaviour patterns in adult life.

If a child is warned against danger in connection with road-safety the child will adopt behaviour in adulthood, which embraces what it has learned.

Furthermore, if our child, perhaps, acquires knowledge by experience – such as putting their hand in the fire – then the hand will be withdrawn at the speed of light by the body's reflex action. Such experiences tend to teach us a lesson, which we seldom forget because the function of the unconscious mind, above all, is to keep us alive at all costs!

Obviously all we are taught at school will be under the control of the unconscious mind. It is said that whatever we learn is, in fact, a learned behaviour because we take in information through our senses, store it in our memory banks and then master a way in which to recall it on demand with accuracy and precision.

This process applies whether we are acquiring facts and knowledge or whether we are developing dexterity in a skill such as driving a car or doing mental arithmetic or playing the piano.

Bodily functions

The unconscious mind is also responsible for keeping us alive by controlling all bodily functions. It, therefore, functions to orchestrate our nervous system, our breathing apparatus, our blood circulatory system, our digestive system, our reproductive system and our hormonal systems.

The unconscious mind controls the working of each of these systems and also keeps in order all the internal organs such as the heart, lungs and stomach which are vital to the efficient functioning of these systems.

The unconscious mind is at work night and day, working 24 hours of the day, to keep our heart beating, controlling our breathing, digesting our food, regulating our body temperature, regenerating new body cells and fighting infection.

SELF-ASSESSMENT QUESTIONS

- What role does the unconscious mind play in the hypnotherapeutic process?

- How would you define the concept of the unconscious mind?

- Can you name some positive emotions and some negative emotions?

- How do we absorb information?

- Why is information stored in our memory?

- What is the relationship between the conscious mind and the unconscious mind with regard to learning?

- How would you define the term repressed memory?

- What is the function of our imagination?

- How do our past experiences affect our current life?

- What bodily functions are controlled by the unconscious mind?

WHAT IS A HYPNOTHERAPIST?

A hypnotherapist is one who utilises the trance-state as a means of giving therapeutic treatment for a range of emotional and psychological disorders. They may deal with anything from simple habit control to conditions of extreme neurotic anxiety.

The role of the hypnotherapist is to guide the client into a trance-state and from there to undertake whatever therapeutic work is required. In fact, it can be said that the therapist is merely a guide or facilitator who allows the client to experience their own state of self-hypnosis.

For this reason, it is often said, therefore, that all hypnosis is self-hypnosis. For successful therapy to occur a relationship will need to be built up between hypnotherapist and client based on mutual consent and trust which can facilitate a free and flowing communication between the two parties. If these conditions are in evidence, the therapist is said to be in **rapport** with the client.

Consider now some thoughts on the role of the hypnotherapist:

Clinical hypnosis is a skill of using words and gestures in particular ways to achieve specific outcomes.
Michael D Yapko
Essentials of Hypnosis

What the hypnotist is interested in is a certain class of changes in the functioning of the mind and body brought about in a non-physical and naturalistic way.
Dylan Morgan
The Principles of Hypnotherapy

The hypnotherapist is trained in hypnotic techniques which may fall into two principal categories and which employ different methods of approach – **clinical therapy** and **analytical therapy**. In practice, of course, the hypnotherapist often works using a combination of both types of therapy. These two branches of hypnotherapy will now be considered separately and in detail.

SELF-ASSESSMENT QUESTIONS

- What is a hypnotherapist?

- What is the role of the hypnotherapist?

- Is it true to say that hypnosis is not a therapy in itself?

- What kind of work does a hypnotherapist do for their clients?

- What needs to occur to ensure that therapy will be successful when working as a hypnotherapist?

- How would you define the term rapport?

CLINICAL HYPNOTHERAPY

Clinical hypnotherapy is used mainly for simple problems and minor disorders but can also be employed to complement other forms of therapy.

Clinical hypnotherapy is also sometimes referred to as suggestive therapy or brief therapy.

Suggestive therapy – as the name implies – utilises the trance-state to implant positive suggestions in the client's unconscious mind in order to allow the client to heal or to derive benefit in some way. For example, suggestive therapy can be used to encourage a smoker to quit the habit or to assist a client to overcome a simple fear or phobic condition.

Brief therapy is so-called because relief from symptoms can usually be achieved in less than 5 sessions.

Let us now consider some typical applications of clinical hypnotherapy.

Smoking cessation

A smoker can help them self to quit smoking easily and effortlessly without any withdrawal symptoms.

The hypnotherapist will suggest to the client that the habit is unnecessary, disgusting and a serious impediment to good health.

Simple phobias

Irrational fears and phobias can provoke anxiety and tension. If a client finds that they are suffering repeatedly and seemingly uncontrollably from such experiences, then the hypnotherapist will be able to assist the client to overcome the problem by tackling it at its source.

With a simple phobia, the subject's accumulated anxiety is triggered by the sight or knowledge of the presence of a specific object. Some common causes of simple fears and phobias might be insects, mice, reptiles, crowds, strangers, heights, water, thunder and doctors.

Weight management

Weight can be controlled or managed effectively and naturally when a client has developed a number of unwanted eating habits. This kind of therapy means that a client can overcome the problem without resorting to drugs or having to endure a stringent diet which might deprive the client of essential nourishment.

Unwanted habits

If a client has developed an irritating or unwanted habit which is anxiety-related, the hypnotherapist will be able to treat this condition. Habits such as nail-biting, hair-pulling, excessive fidgeting and teeth-grinding can usually be eliminated quite easily and very naturally with hypnotherapy. Children can also be treated for habits such as bed-wetting and thumb-sucking with hypnotherapy.

Confidence-building

A lack of confidence and a low self-esteem can inhibit a client's enjoyment of life or impair the chances of success in both personal and professional life.

Hypnotherapy can be used to build up a client's confidence or to raise self-esteem and will eradicate the misery of having to suffer in silence because of conditions such as feelings of inferiority, insecurity, shyness, timidity, indecisiveness, confusion, blushing, stuttering and stammering.

Performance enhancement

Hypnotherapy is helpful in enabling a client to function more efficiently in circumstances which would normally provoke anxiety. Hypnotic techniques can be employed to assist the client in coping with examination nerves, stage-fright, public speaking and to aid the process of accelerated learning, memory-recall and sports or athletics performance.

Pain management

Pain which is psychosomatic in origin can often be assisted under hypnosis as can:

- accelerating the healing process after an injury or following an operation

- accelerating the recovery process when recuperating from a severe illness

- relieving chronic or acute pain

- preparing a patient for surgery or dentistry

- preparing a pregnant woman for childbirth

When hypnotherapy is used for pain management, the therapist will emphasise to the client that the treatment will not entirely remove the pain but will enable the client to cope with it using hypnotic techniques.

Prior to commencing pain management therapy, the client will usually be asked by the therapist to consult a medical practitioner. This request will ensure that the pain is not a warning signal that something is radically wrong with the client which requires them to undergo medical or surgical treatment in order to affect a cure.

Stress management

Stress-related problems can be extremely unpleasant and can be potentially dangerous if a person is subjected to long-term, underlying stress symptoms.

Hypnotherapy can help a client to cope with symptoms such as sleep disturbances, exhaustion, headaches, migraine, skin conditions, digestive disorders, urinary disorders, sexual dysfunction and relationship problems which are stress-related.

The hypnotherapist will teach the client a variety of relaxation techniques and help them to take the pressure out of life as much as possible.

SELF-ASSESSMENT QUESTIONS

- What is clinical hypnotherapy?

- Give some alternatives for the term clinical hypnotherapy.

- In what ways might a clinical hypnotherapist help a client to stop smoking?

- How would you define the term phobia?

- Give some examples of simple phobias.

- Why is weight management using hypnotherapy a natural means of treatment?

- Give some examples of unwanted habits for which a client may seek the help of a hypnotherapist.

- Give some examples of ways in which a lack of confidence may affect an individual.

- In what circumstances might you consult a hypnotherapist for pain management therapy?

- In what ways might an individual be helped by a hypnotherapist when dealing with stress-related problems?

ANALYTICAL HYPNOTHERAPY

Analytical hypnotherapy is employed for investigative psychotherapy or psychoanalytical exploration of the client's problems using hypnosis as a vehicle through which to conduct the treatment.

With this method of therapy, the hypnotherapist is concerned with finding the root-cause of a problem or set of problems by asking the client to look in detail at events and perceptions formed in childhood or early adulthood.

This kind of therapy is often termed hypnoanalysis because it describes the fact that the client is analysing the problem in terms of events and their perception of those events.

Analytical therapy is based on psychoanalysis which was discovered by Sigmund Freud in the latter part of last century and the early part of this century. Today, however, the process, and our understanding of it, has been very much refined and further developed since Freud's time.

Analytical therapy is used to treat clients with emotional problems of a deep-rooted nature. The analytical hypnotherapist, therefore, usually deals with clients who suffer from:

- acute depressive disorders

- compulsive or obsessive conditions

- states of high anxiety such as panic attacks

- severe phobic conditions such as claustrophobia (fear of enclosed spaces), agoraphobia (fear of open spaces) and fears of flying

- eating disorders such as obesity, anorexia or bulimia

- substance abuse such as alcoholism or drug-abuse

- major sexual dysfunction

- the effects on the adult of childhood abuse such as emotional, physical or sexual abuse

The analytical therapist will, of course, treat any client with severe emotional or psychological problems because, in some cases, the client may not be aware of what their problem actually is. As this can sometimes be a painstaking process, the client may be required to attend for several sessions of therapy – certainly at least 6 sessions would be the minimum number required to tackle deep-seated neuroses.

Often, in practice, of course, the client may need to attend for 10 or 20 sessions or more depending on the severity of the case.

All the above-mentioned conditions are regarded as

neurotic conditions which are disorders of the client's personality brought about by some kind of unconscious conflict which can be treated by therapeutic intervention with the help of a therapist.

However, the hypnoanalyst is not able to assist clients with psychotic disorders for which drug treatment or psychiatric treatment is usually required.

In undertaking analytical hypnotherapy, the client is able to take an in-depth view of the whole of their life – as if they were examining it in detail under a microscope. This detailed self-examination allows the client to:

- pinpoint occasions when danger or life-threatening, traumatic experiences beset them.

- identify experiences which caused extremes of emotional response

- understand the way in which the problems were perceived

- identify the occasions when their main character traits were formed

- understand how the past has affected the present in terms of behaviour, motivations and beliefs

- unearth repressed or partially-repressed memories together with the accompanying negative emotions which are associated with such memories

This kind of therapy is undertaken by asking the client in hypnosis to think about their past and particularly childhood where most of our emotional problems will have originated.

The therapist will then ask the client to allow their unconscious mind to relay to the therapist any thoughts, notions, perceptions and meanings which they personally attach to the memories and impressions of these experiences.

This process of freely revealing and uncovering one's thoughts is known as free association.

Free association is also used to allow a client to access a repressed memory which might have been temporarily out of conscious awareness and which is causing the client emotional distress due to unconscious conflict in the mind.

Once repressed memories have surfaced and the accompanying repressed emotion has been discharged, the therapist will then work through such memories in order to help the client to come to terms with the effects of the past experiences.

A discharge of emotion on the client's part indicates to the therapist that some part of the memory which the client is retrieving caused a degree of unconscious conflict in the mind and the effects of this conflict have resulted in the client's current symptoms.

This discharge of emotion is known as an abreaction and

reveals the individual's true response to the situation.

SELF-ASSESSMENT QUESTIONS

- What do you understanding by the term analytical hypnotherapy?

- What are the origins of hypnoanalytical therapy?

- What do you understanding by the term panic attack?

- What types of symptoms can be treated by analytical therapy?

- What is hypnoanalysis likely to entail?

- When a client undergoes hypnoanalysis what kind of information are they likely to discover about themselves?

- What is the process of free association?

- What do you understand by the term abreaction?

MODULE 3
THERAPEUTIC TECHNIQUES

Eliciting client information

Trance-induction

- Physical-relaxation techniques

- Mental-relaxation techniques

- Formal induction techniques

Self-hypnosis

- Self-hypnosis for mental relaxation

- Self-hypnosis for self-empowerment

- Personal preparation for self-hypnosis

Therapeutic suggestion

- Direct and indirect suggestion

- Post-hypnotic suggestion

Therapeutic metaphor

ELICITING CLIENT INFORMATION

At the start of a course of therapy, the hypnotherapist will ask the client a number of questions in order to compile a complete case-history for the client. The therapist will, thus, gain a thorough understanding of the nature of the client's problems. In this way both therapist and client can get to know each other and learn to work together.

The type of information which the therapist will elicit from the client will be:

- personal details such as name, address and telephone number

- the nature of the presenting problem

- the nature of symptoms and the effect of such symptoms

- a brief background medical history

- a record of any medication currently being administered to the client

- a brief family history

- information about close relationships and friendships

- information about other areas of life such as work and leisure-interests

- details of any fears or phobias from which the client may suffer

- details of any regular habit-patterns or behavioural traits to which the client is subject

The therapist will also enquire whether the client is, in fact, a suitable candidate for hypnosis and so information will be sought about whether the client has any heart conditions or epileptic tendencies or a history of psychotic or psychiatric disorders.

If the therapist is in any doubt about a client's suitability for treatment they may refuse to accept the client's case and advise the client to contact their general medical practitioner.

The therapist may also enquire whether the client has any past experience of hypnosis or relaxation techniques. If the client is a newcomer to hypnosis, the therapist may then ask them whether they have good imaginative powers as this attribute is an asset for all hypnosis-subjects.

Furthermore, previous experience of hypnosis and good imaginative resources will mean that the client will be able to practice self-hypnosis successfully in their own time as an adjunct to the therapy.

Because the hypnotherapist is a professional practitioner, it will be important that accurate information is recorded about the client. If you are going to undertake hypnotherapy yourself personally, it will be important for you to feel that you can be totally honest with your therapist when answering such questions.

Should you wish to be referred to a competent therapist, then contact the relevant association.

SELF-ASSESSMENT QUESTIONS

- Why is it necessary for the hypnotherapist to ask a client a number of questions at the start of the therapy?

- What kind of information will a therapist elicit from the client at the start of therapy?

- Why might a therapist ask the client whether they have a heart condition or heart disease?

- If a client were found to have a history of psychiatric disorders, what might the hypnotherapist say to them when this information is revealed?

- Why might a hypnotherapist ask the client whether they have ever experienced hypnosis prior to attending the first therapy session?

TRANCE-INDUCTION

When therapy commences it will be important for the client to learn how to relax and thus to enter the trance-state. The therapist will usually guide the client into the trance-state by using one or more methods of relaxation in order to allow both the mind and the body to relax. Any guidance the therapist may give the client to help them enter the hypnotic state is referred to as a trance-induction.

Physical-relaxation techniques

With this method of relaxation, the client may be asked to relax muscles by a process of tightening and then loosening them in order to release any muscular tension which is being retained by the client.

A typical physical-relaxation process might take the following form:

Therapist: Focus your attention, please, on your feet and squeeze the muscles of your feet as tightly as you possibly can. Hold these muscles very tightly while I count to 3. 1, 2, 3. Now release those feet muscles and, as you do so, allow those muscles to relax and feel the tension just melting away. That's right.

The therapist will then use a similar pattern of wording and work progressively up the body from the feet to the legs, to the stomach, to the chest, to the back, to the arms, to the shoulders, to the neck and, finally, to the head.

It may also be that the therapist will ask the client to co-ordinate their breathing pattern with the physical-relaxation procedure being undertaken.

Mental-relaxation techniques

With this method of relaxation, the client will be encouraged to relax the mind and to switch off from everyday thoughts or problems. By this means, the therapist gives the client suggestions to encourage and to speed up the process of relaxation until the trance-state is achieved.

The therapist may use any of a number of topics in order to induce a relaxed state in the client's mind. The client, therefore, may be asked to visualise a restful scene or a holiday place so that peaceful thoughts can influence the client's state of mind. The technique of creative visualisation is used quite extensively in hypnotherapy.

A typical mental-relaxation process might take the following form:

Therapist: Can you imagine yourself taking a delightful walk in a peaceful place in the country? Perhaps you may be taking a well-trodden path by the side of a stream or through the fields. Look around at all you can see and behold nature in all its infinite beauty. Listen to the songs of the birds or watch the white, fluffy clouds as they float across the blue sky. Or perhaps your path may meander through the woods where you can see the sun shining through the branches and leaves of the trees. And maybe you can feel the soft earth beneath your feet and smell the sweet, fragrant scents and aromas of the grass and the bark of the trees.

Did you notice how this relaxation-process had the effect of enlivening your senses? Stimulating sensory imagery will also be the aim of the hypnotherapist when inducing the trance-state. This is because the unconscious mind is responsible for processing information received through our senses and when the senses are encouraged to relax, then the mind will follow suit.

Formal induction techniques

Sometimes a therapist may use a specific technique which will help the client to enter the trance-state by using an acknowledged method of induction which will speedily induce a hypnotic state.

For example, a client may be asked to fix their gaze on a spot or on an object in the room while the therapist gives the client suggestions for relaxation. Also the therapist may ask the client to concentrate on physical sensations within their body – such as the heaviness or the lightness of their limbs – using this as a focus for the client's attention.

Once the client is relaxed and peaceful, the hypnotic trance-state can then be further enhanced prior to the commencement of the therapy. In order to aid this process, the therapist may use a number of techniques to deepen the trance-state. For example, the therapist may ask the client to imagine walking down some steps or to wander down a long corridor or to pass through a series of doors. If you have personally experienced hypnosis or hypnotherapy, then perhaps you will be able to recall and to identify the techniques which were used in your case.

At the end of the therapeutic session, the therapist will use some means to bring the subject out of the trance-state. For example, the therapist may count from 1 to 5 and then ask the client to open their eyes or alternatively suggestions will be made to the client to revive themselves in order to return to conscious awareness.

SELF-ASSESSMENT QUESTIONS

- What do you understand by the term trance-induction?

- What is the value of physical relaxation with regard to inducing a hypnotic state?

- How might a therapist go about conducting a physical-relaxation session?

- What is the value of mental relaxation with regard to inducing a hypnotic state?

- How might a therapist go about conducting a mental-relaxation session?

- What types of imagery would you personally use to allow your own mind to relax?

- Why do you think it is necessary to be physically and mentally relaxed when undertaking therapy?

- Can you suggest other ways in which the trance-state may be induced with a client?

- How might a hypnotherapist deepen or accelerate the trance-experience with the client?

- How might a hypnotherapist terminate or conclude the trance-experience with a client?

SELF-HYPNOSIS

For certain types of therapy, the hypnotherapist may deem it advisable to teach the client how to undertake self-hypnosis. This will mean that the client can then practice relaxation and creative-visualisation techniques in their own time and at their own pace. If the client is receiving therapy for stress management or pain management, for example, the therapist will be very likely to teach the client self-hypnosis and to ask the client to carry out certain tasks away from the consulting room.

In some cases, the therapist will also give the client an audio recording in order to assist the client with their self-hypnosis work. Often clients who are receiving therapy for weight management or smoking cessation or sports improvement will be given a pre-recorded relaxation to practice between formal sessions.

Self-hypnosis can, of course, be used as a backup to most forms of treatment particularly when undergoing suggestive therapy.

We will now look at ways in which you can improve your life with the aid of self-hypnosis. We give below two typical examples of ways in which hypnotic techniques can be applied to assist you personally with relaxation and self-empowerment. You can utilise and adopt these techniques for your own benefit and self-development.

Self-hypnosis for mental relaxation

In order to relax mentally it will be essential for you to be able to conjure up thoughts and images which would normally have a relaxing effect on your mind. For example, to think about resting on a beach in a holiday resort will bring into your mind thoughts of taking time off and enjoying the warmth of the sun and of getting away from it all. Therefore, you would need to use a form of creative visualisation which will help to induce these kinds of feelings within you.

Your visualisation imagery for mental relaxation, therefore, would need to include the following types of ideas and images:

- preparing for a holiday and the excitement of planning and packing

- feeling the thrill of travelling to a new, unknown or exotic place

- treating yourself – with no expense spared – to the luxury of a getting-away-from-it-all holiday

- taking time out for yourself away from the worries and cares of everyday life

- visiting places of beauty and interest and getting in touch with nature

- being delighted by the sight of breath-taking views and scenes

- admiring the countryside or the mountains or the valleys

- being bathed in the warmth of the sun

- breathing in the fresh and rejuvenating air

If you are able to make a mental record of the types of images you would wish to create for yourself, then a mental-visualisation exercise can be undertaken by you at any time. Alternatively, you could write a brief script of what you want to say to yourself and then, perhaps, record it.

The wording of a typical self-hypnosis script for mental relaxation might, for example, be:

And now lie back and feel your body sinking into the soft, golden sand. Feel it caressing you, soothing you, warming you and healing you. Feel the warmth of the sun on your skin, bringing with it essential nourishment to allow your body to rest and relax. Step off the roundabout of life and allow this holiday to really, really benefit and relax you – free from cares and worries, leaving them all behind. Observe the beauty of nature, be at one with nature. Watch the sea as the tides drift in and out – the natural way. Listen to the plaintive cries of the sea birds, calling to one another. Feel the bracing air caress your cheek and brush through your hair. Breathe in and drink in this atmosphere allowing it to relax you more and more – showing your body simply how to relax naturally.

When you are devising your script for mental relaxation, remember to make it as personal to you as you can. So that if you have ever visited a place in which you felt deliriously happy, rested and contented, then visit that place again in your mind. Alternatively, you may find that using your imagination freely to create the perfect place for a restful holiday is precisely what is required for you.

Self-hypnosis for self-empowerment

In order to empower yourself it will be necessary for you to generate images of challenge, success and advancement. For this you will need to be able to draw on resources which you possess and which you have utilised to your own benefit in the past. For example, think of a time when you accepted a challenge and then were able to carry out that task or project very successfully. If you find it hard to identify a time when you have personally excelled at something, then think of a person whom you know or know of who would easily possess such attributes.

Your visualisation imagery for self-empowerment, therefore, would need to include the following types of ideas and images:

- preparing and planning your project and setting your own standards of achievement

- feeling the excitement at rising to the challenge and of meeting it

- noticing how other people are admiring your talents, your courage, your internal resources, etc

- feeling the joy at being praised and admired

- noticing how flexible and adaptable you are at handling any difficulties or obstacles which might be strewn in your path

- feeling exhilarated at your own success

- feeling overjoyed at how you exceeded even your own expectations

The wording of a typical self-hypnosis script for self-empowerment might, for example, be:

Imagine yourself standing at the helm of a ship on the high seas and watching the elements around you. Notice how the ship rises and falls with the swell of the sea just as your chest rises and falls as you breathe. Get in contact with these natural elements and take the power from nature in the raw in all its inspiring glory.

Allow this power to embrace you, surround you and encompass you until you are at one with the mighty power of the sea, the tides, the wind and the sky. Capture these resources and take them into your everyday life. Utilise this power and strength within you.

Allow it to guide you when taking decisions, communicating with people, going about your daily work. Harness this strength to empower you and to take you forward in life to achieve that goal which you know you can conquer.

Remember to personalise your script in order to tap into those parts of nature or the universe which are appropriate and relevant for you. Use such a script to enhance or to encourage the development of your own natural resources so that you can take yourself forward in life with confidence and optimism.

Personal preparation for self-hypnosis

Once you have chosen your topic, devised your strategy, written out and, possibly, recorded your self-hypnosis script, then you will need to prepare yourself suitably for a self-induced hypnotic state.

To induce self-hypnosis, you will need to take the following steps:

- select a time during which you will be unlikely to be disturbed for about half an hour when you are alone switch off the phone

- lie down on a bed or a comfortable chair

- close your eyes, uncross your legs and let your arms hang loosely at your sides

- take one or two deep, relaxing breaths

- allow your body to relax – perhaps using a physical-relaxation technique in order to achieve this

- Now play your audio recording or carry out your own creative-visualisation exercise.

You could also practice this exercise with a close friend who might also be willing to read your script to you at the appropriate time.

You might also wish to play some relaxing music while doing your creative-visualisation exercises or while having it read to you.

SELF-ASSESSMENT QUESTIONS

1. What do you understand by the term self-hypnosis?

2. What do you understand by the term creative visualisation?

3. What kind of mental images might you utilise when undertaking creative visualisation for mental relaxation?

4. What kind of mental images might you utilise when undertaking creative visualisation for self-empowerment?

5. What kind of physical sensations and feelings might you utilise when undertaking creative visualisation for self-empowerment?

6. In what other ways might self-hypnosis be used to help you personally?

7. How would you go about preparing yourself for a self-hypnosis session?

8. What might be the value of asking a friend to assist you with self-hypnosis?

9. What is the value of self-hypnosis as an adjunct to therapy?

10. List the ways in which self-hypnosis could be used as an adjunct to therapeutic treatment.

THERAPEUTIC SUGGESTION

Having considered the type of treatment which a hypnotherapist can provide, let us now turn our attention to the means by which the therapist performs their work.

Every human being will, in some way, be susceptible to suggestion although some are more so than others. We have all, at one time, been influenced by advertising or swayed by public opinion. We often tend to go with the flow of things rather than wish to stand out from the crowd by being different. It is, therefore, a natural, human trait to be open to suggestion. For this reason, beneficial suggestion is often utilised by the hypnotherapist to encourage the client to heal them self or to expose them self to creative or innovative thinking.

The therapist may, therefore, suggest to a client the benefits of breaking a habit or the advantages of taking care of them self. The therapist specialises in delivering only beneficial and life-enhancing suggestions and, often, the client will seize upon those suggestions which are of special relevance to their case and to their own particular problems.

Direct and indirect suggestion

Suggestions may be delivered by the therapist either in a direct way or in an indirect way. Direct suggestion usually addresses the conscious mind while indirect suggestions are more likely to be accepted by the unconscious mind.

Examples of direct suggestions for trance-induction might be:

Please close your eyes, now.

I want you to focus on your breathing pattern.

Let your unconscious mind wander into the past.

Allow yourself to become completely relaxed.

Examples of indirect suggestions for trance-induction might be:

I wonder if you can feel comfortable with our eyes closed?

Perhaps you can focus for a while on your breathing pattern.

Some hypnotic subjects find that their limbs become light or become heavy when in trance.

The unconscious mind knows everything that it needs to know to resolve your problem for you.

Post-hypnotic suggestion

In many cases the hypnotherapist will make judicious use of the technique known as post-hypnotic suggestion. With this technique the therapist will make a request of the client to perform a task or to adopt a style of behaviour which will apply once the client has emerged from the trance-state.

Examples of therapeutic post-hypnotic suggestions might be:

And the next time you are offered a cigarette, you will find yourself saying 'NO THANKS, I'M A NON-SMOKER'.

And maybe you will not feel the need to indulge your habit further in the future.

And the very next time you sit in that chair, you will feel yourself beginning to relax still further, still deeper into that wonderful trance-like state.

Note: Everything that is said in a therapeutic setting is a suggestion.

SELF-ASSESSMENT QUESTIONS

1. What do you understand by the term therapeutic suggestion?

2. In what ways are individuals susceptible to suggestion in everyday life?

3. In what ways have you been susceptible to suggestion in the past?

4. Can you distinguish between direct and indirect suggestion?

5. Give some examples of direct and indirect suggestions which might be used in hypnotherapy.

6. What do you understand by the term post-hypnotic suggestion?

7. Give some examples of post-hypnotic suggestions.

8. If you have personally undertaken hypnotherapy, what types of suggestions were made to you by your therapist?

THERAPEUTIC METAPHOR

A therapeutic metaphor is an indirect means of conveying a message to a hypnotherapy client by relating a story. The therapist will tell a story with a special message contained within it which is particularly applicable to the client.

The use of metaphor is an indirect means of influencing the client and was a technique widely used by one of the world's acknowledged experts on hypnotherapy, Dr Milton Erickson (1901-1980). Erickson was a master of the use of indirect techniques to assist his clients – of which the metaphor was one of the principal means.

A metaphor is an indirect means of communication because often the client is not consciously aware of what is being conveyed. Sometimes the client will be required to make a contribution of their own when unravelling the meaning of the metaphor.

By this means the metaphor is left open-ended so that the client can adapt the message embedded within it to fit the particular circumstances. Metaphors will often be suitably vague in this respect because it is for the client to make the unconscious changes and to supply the appropriate missing piece of the jigsaw puzzle.

An example of a metaphor to assist a client with the process of changing habits or thinking patterns might include a description of the changing seasons. A typical metaphor of this type might be:

Now let us think of autumn. That season of rich yellows, oranges, reds and browns. That season when the leaves change colour and fall down from the trees. Perhaps you can see a leaf spiralling down from a branch of a tree being carried on the wind to the ground? Sometimes we can hear the crackle of the dead leaves underfoot as we tread that well-worn path. This is the time of year when the little furry creatures begin to prepare for the coming of winter, lining their nests and storing up food for the winter.

And in the wintertime we reflect by the flickering fireside – full of hope, expectation and readiness for the coming of spring. The daffodil trumpets in the beginning of spring. The tiny snowdrop and the delicate crocus push their way through the hard earth – full of vigour and determination and eagerly awaiting the freshness and newness of the coming season. And every creature in the land is aware of these changes automatically and without knowing it. There is an inevitability about the times and seasons which all creatures instinctively know. The birds know about migration although no-one tells them. The squirrel somehow knows to forage for and bury nuts even though no-one tells him. Strange the ways of nature, aren't they?

In this metaphor images of inevitable change, of preparation and of newness are being put forward to assist the client with their process of change but without actually specifying that this is what is required of them.

The therapist will also need to listen for phrases used by

the client which depict their opinion of the world and their outlook on life. In this way the therapist will be able to discover the client's metaphor for life and thus understand how the client views the world. Examples of a metaphor about life might be:

Life is a merry go round.

Life is a pain.

There are never enough hours in the day.

There are traffic-jams everywhere you go.

SELF-ASSESSMENT QUESTIONS

1. What do you understand by the term therapeutic metaphor?

2. Who was Milton Erickson and what contribution did he make to modern hypnotherapy?

3. What is the purpose of a metaphor and in what ways can this purpose be achieved?

4. Give an example of a metaphor which could be used to assist you personally in improving your life.

5. Give some examples of your metaphors for life.

MODULE 4
COUNSELLING TECHNIQUES

CONTENTS

Belief restructuring

- How we acquire beliefs

- Negative beliefs

- Pinpointing techniques

- Gold Counselling techniques

Stress management counselling

- What is stress?

- The fight-or-flight response

- Positive and negative stress

- Relieving stress

BELIEF RESTRUCTURING

One of the most important functions of the hypnotherapist will be to change, alter or modify their client's negative, limiting or destructive beliefs. Such beliefs will be an impediment to the client's progress in both clinical and analytical therapy and so the therapist will utilise their knowledge of belief restructuring to assist and to empower the client.

How we acquire beliefs

As we grow up we learn from others about us. In infancy we learn from our parents or guardians. At play we learn from our siblings or our friends. At school we learn from our teachers and our schoolmates. The aim of all education should be to equip us for life. For example, we learn how to behave so that we may take our place in society, we acquire knowledge and skills so that we may take up a profession or enjoy a leisure-time activity and we learn to be aware of danger so that we can protect ourselves from harm. During this learning process we acquire certain beliefs about ourselves, about others, about the world and about society.

Negative beliefs

All our childhood learning should – in an ideal world – be positive learning and should be to our benefit. However, as we grow – and proceed through the learning process – we may also acquire negative learning and negative beliefs along the way. For example, when a child is frequently told "Don't to that!" or "Stop that!", then they gain a negative learning or a negative belief about their actions or performance or abilities. Similarly if a child is told to "Take care!" or to "Be careful!", then they learn to feel fear and to expect danger.

Unfortunately, some children are taught to believe that they are useless or incapable or incompetent – perhaps by a parent who them self feel in some way inadequate. If such beliefs are acquired at an early age and this learning is then reinforced, the consequences can be detrimental when the individual reaches adulthood.

In these cases, negative beliefs are implanted and ingrained in the child's unconscious mind at a time when they are most susceptible to suggestion and influence. What we learn in childhood is carried with us for the rest of our life until such mistaken beliefs can be resolved in a therapeutic context.

Negative beliefs can, for example, cause a person to:

- lack confidence

- lack motivation

- have a poor self-image

- be overly fearful or anxious

- develop self-punishing or health-hazardous habits

- take unnecessary risks which may endanger life, health or financial security

Therefore, it will be one of the prime concerns of the hypnotherapist to understand what the client's beliefs are and to eliminate, rectify or modify them accordingly in order to assist the client with psychological development.

Pinpointing techniques

This is a simple technique which is used when the specific, root-cause of a problem can be easily identified together with the accompanying beliefs. Pinpointing techniques are usually employed when undertaking clinical hypnotherapy. For example:

A smoking-cessation client might be asked to identify the time when they first started to smoke in order to highlight the reasons for the client's habit

A phobic client might be asked to identify the occasion on which they first experienced the fear for a given object or situation in order to help the client to understand the reasons for their fears.

Gold Counselling techniques

Gold Counselling is a specifically-structured approach to identifying and revising a client's negative, destructive and life-inhibiting beliefs.

With the Gold Counselling method of belief restructuring the client is asked to write a list of personal beliefs on a given topic – usually chosen by the therapist or counsellor.

The client is then asked to link these beliefs together in a specific way in order to identify the belief which is most detrimental to them and on which other beliefs may depend. The counsellor is then able to help the client to understand the root-cause of these beliefs and to resolve them in a satisfactory way.

Here is an example of the way in which Gold Counselling techniques may be applied in a therapeutic context.

A client is asked to write a list of beliefs on the topic of Motivation. The client produces a list and then links each item on the list so that the beliefs can be recorded in both written and pictorial form as given below:

MOTIVATION

A	I have difficulty motivating myself	D
B	I can never find the time	A
C	Upsetting	F
D	Afraid	A
E	Never have enough enthusiasm	C
F	I can never be at peace	D

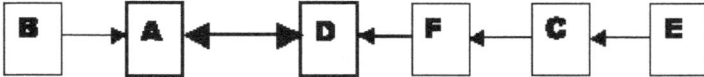

From this information, the counsellor can now deduce that the client's primary beliefs centre on I HAVE DIFFICULTY MOTIVATING MYSELF and AFRAID in connection with their beliefs about personal motivation.

The therapist or counsellor would now set about pinpointing where, when and how the client learned to believe what they believe about motivation. Once the exact root-cause of the problem has been identified and isolated, the therapist would then ask the client:

- whether the original belief was their own – in many cases a negative belief is one held by another person

- whether the original belief is still relevant to the client's life today

- whether the original belief is still valid or appropriate in today's context

In most cases, the counsellor will discover that the negative belief was given to the client inappropriately at some time in the past and need no longer impair the client's life in the present. For example, a belief that you were bad at sums at school may merely be the teacher's opinion – which was not necessarily valid – at a given time in the past. Or perhaps the fact that you were not that good at arithmetic at school is really of no consequence in adult-life today.

Gold Counselling is a widely used therapeutic tool which was created by Georges Philips and developed with Lyn Philips.

SELF-ASSESSMENT QUESTIONS

1. What is the importance of belief restructuring in the therapeutic context?

2. How do we acquire beliefs?

3. List some of the positive beliefs that you hold.

4. List some of the negative beliefs that you hold.

5. In what ways can negative beliefs affect an individual?

6. What do you understand by the term pinpoint therapy?

7. What is Gold Counselling therapy used for?

8. Briefly describe how Gold Counselling can be used to assist a hypnotherapy client with negative beliefs.

STRESS MANAGEMENT COUNSELLING

Stress is a modern buzz-word the treatment of which has now become a major part of the hypnotherapist's work and, therefore, deserves special mention in its own right.

What is stress?

Stress occurs in an individual when an inordinate amount of pressure is put on the resources of that individual and the result is mental and physical overload. Stress, therefore, is both a physical condition and an emotional response to what is perceived as pressure, threat or danger. The object over which an individual can become stressed is known as a stressor.

It should be emphasised, however, that we all react to stress in our own unique and individual ways. For example, what one person regards as stressful another would describe as challenging or exciting or comforting.

Here are some examples of ways in which a person may perceive events as either stressful or not:

- a roller-coast ride could instil fear or generate excitement

- a ring on your doorbell could evoke panic if you were expecting the bailiffs to repossess your home or engender wild excitement if you were expecting to receive a big cheque because you had just won the lottery

- a new baby in the family could be a long-hoped-for joy or a source of financial worry

- a redundancy package could bring relief if you hated your job and had just been offered another much better one or it could mean utter despondency and financial ruin

The important point to note here, therefore, is that we are all individuals who view identical life-events in a range of different ways according to the way in which such events affect us and which types of emotions are evoked.

The fight-or-flight response

The effect of any kind of stress – whether it is positive or negative – will manifest itself as a physical and emotional condition which is related to our instinctive drives and inner needs for self-preservation. Stress is registered both in physical and emotional terms in human beings by what is known as the fight-or-flight response.

The fight-or-flight response occurs when an individual perceives pressure, threat or danger for which they are ill-equipped and their immediate, instinctive response will be either to run away or to stay and fight the impending danger. This response is the same one that helped the caveman to fight off the wild beast or to slay it for food or to run away from the creature in order to stay alive.

The fight-or-flight response is a primitive mechanism but it is necessary for our survival because, firstly, it is the only facility we have and, secondly, we need these resources to be able to defend our life should the occasion ever to arise.

In today's society, of course, we are seldom, if ever, required to face life-threatening danger but the fight-or-flight mechanism is still evoked whenever threat is perceived. Most of the perceived threat, of course, will be of a psychological nature even though a primarily physical reaction is triggered.

With the fight-or-flight response the body's resources spring into action in a split second in the following ways:

- our breathing-rate increases in order to take in fresh supplies of oxygen

- our heart-rate increases in order to pump oxygenated blood around the body

- stress-hormones and chemicals such as adrenaline, cholesterol and thyroxine are released into the bloodstream to boost metabolism and to stimulate the blood circulatory system

- cortisol is released into the bloodstream to help prevent allergic reactions in the event of injury

- endorphins are released into the bloodstream to help kill any pain which may occur as a result of injury

- our digestive system and our reproductive
  system are shut down, slowed down or
  interrupted

- our senses become over-stimulated in order to
  alert us to danger and in readiness for taking the
  appropriate action

From these examples, it can be seen that the
unconscious mind is working overtime and the body is
fully stimulated to react accordingly. The problem arises
when the body is continually subjected to this degree of
over-stimulation for long periods of time unrelentingly.

This, of course, is the danger-point when the body's
systems may pack up as a result of having been
overworked for too long. Thus, heart-diseases, strokes,
arteriosclerosis, ulcers, cancer and a complete mental
and physical breakdown can be the result of the long-
term effects of unchecked stress.

Positive and negative stress

Because we all perceive life's events in different ways,
we can regard stress as either positive or negative.

Positive stress occurs when the individual is excited or
challenged or pleasantly stimulated in some way.
Positive stress is also sometimes referred to as eustress
– a term devised by Professor Hans Seyle who was the
first person to research into the phenomenon and to

publish his research in the 1970s.

Examples of occasions when one might experience positive stress or regard events as positive stressors might be:

- winning the lottery or inheriting some money

- having a new baby

- getting married or meeting a new partner

- getting a new job

- moving house

- going on holiday

Negative stress, on the other hand, occurs when the individual experiences an unpleasant feeling or set of emotions. In this case, negative stress becomes distress for the person concerned.

Examples of occasions when one might suffer from negative stress or regard events as negative stressors might be:

- losing a job or getting demoted

- having continual financial worries

- enduring emotional strife in the family or home environment

- suffering bereavement or the loss of a loved-one

- having ill-health or a disability

- being robbed, burgled or attacked

- living in an unpleasant neighbourhood or in disagreeable circumstances

- being a victim of environmental pollution

Relieving stress

The stress management counsellor will help the client to overcome stress by employing a number of techniques which will alleviate problems and help the client to cope with the stress-inducing situation or circumstances.

Stress-reduction techniques which the therapist will use with their client are:

- mental relaxation techniques such as creative visualisation

- meditative techniques such as counting breaths and clearing the mind of extraneous matter

- physical relaxation techniques

The stress management counsellor will also advise the clients to ensure that a healthy diet and a healthy programme of exercise are maintained in order to resolve the physical effects of the fight-or-flight response.

The stressed client will also receive counselling to ensure that, if possible, circumstances can be altered or remedied and that the client's perception of events can be successfully changed in such a way that the impending threat is averted.

SELF-ASSESSMENT QUESTIONS

1. How would you define the term stress?

2. What role does perception play in stress-related problems?

3. What is a stressor?

4. What is the fight-or-flight mechanism?

5. What are the physical effects of the fight-or-flight response?

6. What do you understand by the term eustress and who first introduced this term into our language?

7. Can you give some examples of positive stressors?

8. Can you give some examples of negative stressors?

9. In what ways can stress usually be relieved?

10. How can the stress management counsellor assist a client in managing stress and combating negative stress?

MODULE 5
SELF-DEVELOPMENT TECHNIQUES

CONTENTS

Neuro-linguistic programming

- General principles of NLP

- Representational systems

- Anchoring

- Reframing

Positive thinking

- Positive affirmations

- Negative self-talk

Assertiveness

- What is assertiveness?

- How is assertiveness employed in practice?

Further study

NEURO-LINGUISTIC PROGRAMMING

Neuro-linguistic programming (or NLP) is a range of therapeutic techniques which have been collected together and documented to allow the practitioner to utilise language patterns and behavioural models to effect therapeutic change in the client.

NLP was developed by John Grinder and Richard Bandler in the early 1970s based on the work of therapists Fritz Perls, Virginia Satir and Milton Erickson. By studying (or *modelling*) the work of these three therapists, Grinder and Bandler were able to ascertain the specific linguistic skills, behaviour and supporting beliefs which each utilised in their therapeutic work. From this research NLP techniques were devised and documented to assist other therapists and practitioners.

Let us now look at some of these techniques which NLP practitioners use and examine how such practices can be utilised for self-development and self-improvement.

General principles of NLP

NLP takes as a premise the fact that the mind can only hold a certain amount of information at one time because of limited energy resources. For this reason, the wealth of information which we absorb into our unconscious mind through our senses minute by minute is – for the sake of expediency – deleted, distorted or generalised to enable us to absorb and store only that which is vital at any given moment. For example, we might look at a scene and only take in certain bits of information about it – the rest will then be condense or abbreviated to prevent the mind from being overloaded.

Furthermore, NLP presupposes that we all view the world from our own individual perspective which tends to influence and colour our thoughts, behaviour and motivations.

In order to be an effective therapist, the NLP practitioner is taught the importance of gaining and maintaining a rapport with a client. This relationship is important in order to be able to guide the client towards realising goals and maximising potential by tapping into their own internal resources.

For this the practitioner needs to observe and monitor the client closely and to be flexible and adaptable in the approach to working with that individual.

Representational systems

All information which the unconscious mind processes is represented in some way via our 5 sensory systems.

These sensory systems are known collectively as our representational systems because it is through these systems that we represent our experiences of the world.

These representational systems are:

visual – sight

auditory – hearing

kinaesthetic – touch/feel

olfactory – smell

gustatory – taste

It has been found that each person is likely to have a tendency towards using one system more than any of the others. So, for example, an individual may rely on using the visual sense more than, say, the auditory or kinaesthetic sense. The visual person, thus, will be good at visualising pictures in the mind's eye and will be more likely to remember pictorial details of events. This system is then known as the individual's **primary** system of representation.

It has also been discovered that our primary representational system is the one to which we refer in our everyday speech by using the words and phrases which depict this system.

The visually-oriented person, therefore, is likely to use words and phrases such as:

I see what you mean.

Keep me in the picture?

The auditory-oriented person is likely to use words and phrases such as:

Can I sound you out on this problem?

I hear what you say.

The kinaesthetically-based person is likely to use words and phrases such as:

How do you feel about this?

I am a bit touchy about this.

It has also been observed that when recalling information or imagining things, the individual will tend to look in a given direction. For example, when a person recalls an event they are likely to look to their right but while reconstructing a scene from the imagination, that same individual will look to their left. This is the kind of information which the therapist will monitor in order to understand the client's thought patterns.

Anchoring

Milton Erickson was a firm believer in the doctrine that an individual has within all the resources they need to effect their own cure or remedy. It is from this premise that the technique of anchoring was developed.

Anchoring is the association of an internal resource or attribute with a sensory image which often brings about an immediate response or behaviour-pattern. For example, a police siren is often an auditory anchor which may be associated with what you believe about the police or an anchor which prompts you to pull your car into the curb or an anchor which triggers you to be vigilant. Similarly, the smell of freshly-baked bread or freshly-ground coffee being brewed is an olfactory anchor which accesses images of comfort and security.

In therapeutic terms, the NLP practitioner would endeavour to anchor positive emotions, attributes and resources in the client which can be utilised for the client's benefit. For example, if a client required some help with feeling confident when dealing with people at work, the therapist might ask the client to remember a time when they felt confident and at ease. The client would then be asked to find a way to preserve (*anchor*) the feelings and emotions which are experienced in the past so that they can regenerate (*fire*) them on demand when such resources are required in the future.

- The anchoring process might be carried out as follows:

- the client is asked to remember – in as much detail as possible using all the senses – the time when they had the required resources or attributes

- the client is then encouraged to feel the feelings, resources or attributes that they had at that specific time as strongly as possible

---

- the client is then asked to capture these feelings by carrying out some kind of physical action such as clenching a fist or squeezing the thumb and forefinger together

- the client is then asked to imagine a different time and place in their imagination when the relevant resources would be needed in the future

- the client is then asked to fire the anchor to bring on-stream the relevant resources in the new situation

By undertaking this process, the client is not only ridding them self of unwanted feelings and negative attitudes but also they are becoming empowered by projecting into the future and proving that the appropriate responses can, in fact, be made in a new situation.

Reframing

Reframing is a means of changing an individual's perception of a problem in order to allow the freedom to live in harmony with them self. Reframing means, literally, putting a new frame around an old picture in order to view it differently and, thus, transform it from being a problem into being a solution.

The hypnotherapist will always seek to help a client by questioning the client in order to discover the client's perspective of any given problem. Often the hypnotherapist can then suggest an alternative view which the client had not previously considered.

For example, if a female client were to view herself as the family doormat, the hypnotherapist would encourage her to voice this fact to the family and then would invite the client to plan ways in which other members of the family could contribute to the running of the home. In this way the client would be invited to view herself as the leader of the orchestra rather than the slave of it.

If a client were to complain of having too many demanding customers at work, for example, then the therapist would endeavour to make the client aware that business was thriving. The client could then take immediate steps to delegate responsibility to junior employees or to take on extra staff to help with the workload. It should be emphasised here that the role of the therapist is certainly not to give advice but to encourage the client to undertake some creative thinking in order to tackle the problem head-on by viewing it differently in some way.

SELF-ASSESSMENT QUESTIONS

1. How would you define the term **neuro-linguistic programming**?

2. Who was responsible for developing NLP?

3. What are the general assumptions on which the theory of NLP is based?

4. What is an anchor?

5. What does the process of anchoring and firing anchors entail?

6. What do you understand by the term reframing?

7. Can you give some examples of occasions when a hypnotherapist would seek to undertake reframing with a client?

8. Can you suggest some ways in which you personally could benefit from anchoring and reframing therapy techniques?

POSITIVE THINKING

Part of the hypnotherapist's work will be to encourage the client to adopt a positive attitude to life and to instil positive thinking.

The aim of positive thinking is to alter negative and destructive thinking patterns and to replace these with beneficial, harmonious, forward-looking and optimistic thoughts and behaviour patterns.

The advantages of positive thinking for the client are that:

- negative habits can gradually be altered by adopting a positive attitude

- positive attitudes to therapy will assist the client's progress

- negative thinking can be overridden or counteracted

Positive thinking, of course, often involves a major shift in the client's personal attitudes and in their attitude to life.

The value of positive thinking is that what we confidently expect to happen will occur because of the mechanics of the natural *Law of Expectation* and the self-fulfilling prophecy. The *Law of Expectation* has such force because of the power that the unconscious mind has to grab hold of an idea or notion and then to make it happen by some means.

Positive thinking is achieved by concentrated effort to the exclusion of all else. Therefore, if we regularly dwell on positive thoughts and banish negative thinking we are brainwashing the mind into adopting new patterns of behaviour and recharging our emotional batteries.

You will, of course, remember that negative beliefs and negative learning is usually installed in the mind when we are in childhood. Therefore, these patterns can be reversed by the adoption of positive thinking and the banishment of negative thinking in later life.

The principal ways in which positive thinking can be achieved is by using positive affirmations and eliminating negative self-talk.

Positive affirmations

Positive affirmations are statements and phrases which convince the unconscious mind that its outlook on life needs to be positive rather than negative. The key to affirmations is that they need to be truisms. They must be meant or they will fail.

Examples of positive-thinking phrases are:

I look forward to a successful and productive day

I am in control of my life

I accept every day as it comes

I feel happy and healthy

I am able to relax and to devote time to myself regularly

When constructing a positively-worded affirmation, the following general rules should be kept in mind:

- use wording which is positive rather than negative (eg *I am* or *I will* rather than *I am not* or *I will not*)

- always state your affirmation in the first person singular and in the present tense (eg *I think positively* rather than *One can think positively*)

- select topics which have a high negative, emotional content (eg worry, lack of control, fear)

- repeat constantly with dedication and commitment to the task

Negative self-talk

At the same time as adopting positive thinking and affirming your thinking, it will be necessary for you to banish negative self-talk as an integral part of the positive-thinking process.

Negative self-talk phrases are those phrases which we often find ourselves saying with our inner voice and which have a limiting or destructive effect on our life.

Such phrases are often the outward manifestation of our negative emotions – our fears, our guilt and our feelings of being unworthy or undeserving.

Examples of negative-self talk are:

I can't …

I'm afraid that …

I ought to …

I must …

I should never …

I am really sorry …

I am useless at …

The hypnotherapist will often need to draw the client's attention to the fact that such phrases are dominating the client's speech. Often merely being aware of such negative self-talk will serve to initiate the process of eliminating negative thinking.

SELF-ASSESSMENT QUESTIONS

- How would you define the term positive thinking?

- What are the advantages of adopting positive thinking in your daily life?

- Can you give some examples of positive affirmations which you could adopt in your life?

- What general rules would you adhere to when devising positive affirmations?

- What is negative self-talk?

- How is negative thinking installed in the mind?

- Can you give some examples of negative self-talk to which you are personally prone?

- How would you propose to eliminate such negative thinking from your mind?

ASSERTIVENESS

The hypnotherapist will also aim to teach the client self-assertiveness as an adjunct to therapeutic intervention.

For the client who is lacking in confidence or who suffers from a lack of self-worth, assertiveness training will often be an integral part of therapy. Practising being self-assertive will encourage the client to restore the necessary balance and harmony into their life and into interactions with others.

What is assertiveness?

Assertiveness entails adopting a balanced mode of behaviour when communicating and interacting with others.

Adopting assertive behaviour, therefore, means that:

- you take a balanced, middle-of-the-road approach to human interaction

- you take a calm, rational stance to life in which you are in control of yourself and your behaviour

- you freely acknowledge and express your feelings and needs

- you respect and acknowledge the feelings and rights of others

Embracing assertive techniques and behaviour will put

the client on the road to securing confidence, self-worth and a good self-image.

Being assertive, however, does not mean being aggressive, passive or manipulative when the individual is in a confrontational situation.

Being *aggressive* may manifest itself when an individual is overbearing, patronising, bullying or self-righteous. The aggressive person will usually be prone to temper tantrums and will insist on getting their own way at the expense of others. Often such behaviour will mean that the aggressive person will isolate them self from those with whom they are desperately trying to communicate.

Being *passive* may manifest itself when an individual becomes submissive, obliging, self-deprecating or sycophantic. The passive individual is likely to be withdrawn and will opt out of taking responsibility for decision-making which may in itself, lead them to become resentful of and frustrated by others.

Being *manipulative* may manifest itself when an individual uses indirect means to fulfil their needs. Manipulative traits fall between being too aggressive and being too passive. The manipulative individual will be the martyr or the hypochondriac in society who seeks to satisfy their wants by emotionally blackmailing others.

How is assertiveness employed in practice?

Assertiveness entails knowing how to behave appropriately, knowing one's human rights and putting this knowledge into practice.

The assertive individual will appreciate their own human rights and the rights of interaction with other people. For example, the assertive individual will be able to:

- directly state their needs and wants

- act in a responsible manner giving consideration to the needs of others as appropriate

- feel free to express emotions if they are hurt, deceived, exploited or abused in any way

- take decisions without the permission or approval of others

- set their own priorities and boundary limitations as they deem fit

- give themselves permission to make mistakes and to change their own mind

Taking this attitude of mind and this approach to life will enable the individual to focus on themselves as a person in their own right – thus taking a balanced outlook on life and fostering harmonious communications with others.

The assertive individual will, therefore, become emotionally stable, well-balanced and of a happy disposition. They will not be a slave either to their past or to the dictates of those with whom they interact on a daily basis.

When interacting with others – particularly in confrontational situations or circumstances of potential conflict – the assertive individual will not procrastinate, will be forthright, rational and will act appropriately.

SELF-ASSESSMENT QUESTIONS

- How would you describe assertive behaviour?

- What is the benefit of adopting assertiveness techniques, attitudes and behaviours?

- How would you describe an aggressive individual?

- What character traits are likely to be exhibited by a passive individual?

- Do you personally know anyone who is manipulative by nature?

- How would you endeavour to be more assertive in your life?

Congratulations

You have completed the Hypnotherapy Foundation Course and are now better able to decide if hypnotherapy is the profession for you to follow.

Enjoy your journey.

Georges and Lyn Philips

FURTHER STUDY

Now that you have completed your work on the **Hypnotherapy Foundation Course**, it may be time to consider further study in the light of your new-found knowledge.

For those students who wish to investigate the topic of therapeutic hypnosis further or seek to become qualified please visit our website for further information.

For those students with an interest in aspects of stress management, the **Stress Management an introduction for professionals** will enable you to gain further knowledge and specialise in this field.

Please visit our website for further details.
www.georgesphilips.com/MPRH

Further information may be found at:

UK

The Hypnotherapy Society
The National Hypnotherapy Register

USA

The American Association of Professional
Hypnotherapists
The Association for Professional Hypnosis and
Psychotherapy

For an example of certified hypnotherapy training in the
UK visit Jacquelyne Morisons website at
http://www.jmht.co.uk

ESSENTIAL READING

You are advised to purchase the following books to assist you with your studies if you are interested in developing a deeper understanding.

Positive Thinking
Vera Peiffer
ISBN 978-0007130993

Self-Hypnosis: The Complete Manual for Health and Self-Change
Dr Brian M Alman and Dr Peter Lambrou
ISBN 978-0876306505

Essentials Of Hypnosis (Basic Principles Into Practice)
Michael D. Yapko, Ph.D.,
ISBN 978-0876307618

The Art of Hypnotherapy
Roy Hunter MS
ISBN 978-1845904401

My Little Book of N L P – Neuro Linguistic Programming (e-book)
Georges Philips and Tony Jennings
ASIN B005DMURYY

My Little Book of Verbal Antidotes (e-book)
Georges Philips and Tony Jennings
ASIN: B005Z1XGMS

My Little Book of Meditation (e-book)
Georges Philips and Tony Jennings
ASIN: B005Z1XCG8

Mental and Physical Relaxation with Hypnosis – Audio (Original classics series)
Georges Philips
Free Audio Download (available for a limited period)

Recommended reading

For those students who wish to study the subject in greater depth, we would recommend that you may also wish to purchase the following books.

Change Directions
Georges Philips
ISBN 978-1904928003

Gold Counselling: A Practical Psychology with NLP
Georges Philips and Lyn Buncher (Philips)
ISBN 1899836063

Principles of NLP
Joseph O'Connor and Ian McDermot
ISBN 978-1855383449

Analytical Hypnotherapy: Vol. 1: Theoretical Principles
Jacquelyne A. Morison – Georges Philips
ISBN 978-1899836772

Analytical Hypnotherapy: Vol. 2: Practical Applications
Jacquelyne A. Morison – Georges Philips
ISBN 978-1845904074

Rapid Cognitive Therapy
Georges Philips and Terence Watts
ISBN 978-1899836376

Stress management – A Course for Professionals.
Georges Philips and Simon Shawcross
ISBN 978-1-904928-06-5

Seminars, Workshops and Lectures of Milton H. Erickson: Healing in Hypnosis v. 1
Milton H. Erickson
ISBN 978-1853434051

Handbook of Hypnotic Suggestions and Metaphors
D. Corydon Hammond
ISBN 978-0393700954

DVD's and CD

Hypnotic Inductions and Deepening Techniques
Georges Philips
ASIN 0953666786

Hypnotic Inductions and Post Hypnotic Suggestions
Georges Philips
ASIN 0953666794

Background Music

Indirect Trance Volume 1 A
Hypno -Tec – Georges Philips
There are several unique features included within the music. The recording incorporates the use of a heartbeat that begins at 78 beats per minute and reduces to 45 beats per minute within a 20-minute period.

In addition the looped music, though seemingly repetitious, creates a time distortion due to its cyclic nature. This is achieved by giving the appearance that the tempo is unchanging where in fact there is an ever-increasing cycle. The instruments used encourage the use of deep breathing to enhance calm. Playing time 51minutes
ISBN 978-1-904928-07-2

www.ingramcontent.com/pod-product-compliance
Lightning Source LLC
Chambersburg PA
CBHW030021290326
41934CB00005B/433